DOCTOR ETHEL BARKING'S
ENGLAND

Written by Martin Morris

Designed and Illustrated by Peter Searle

Doctor Barking's archive materials kindly
made available by Matthew May of Camden Town.

Doctor Barking's Wardrobe courtesy
Mr Bruce Allen of the Antipodes

This (very valuable) First Edition of Freddie
Farquar's 'Naughty but Nice' Series published 1999 by
The Dog's Rollocks Ideas Co Ltd.,
Timbers, Milford Road, Elstead, Godalming, Surrey
GU8 6HZ, England.

Tel/Fax: +44 (0) 1252 702754.
Mobile: +44 (0) 468 627344.

The complete Dog's Rollock's range is available on the web:

www.dogs-rollocks.com

Printed in UK.

Doctor Ethel Barking's ENGLAND
A catalogue record for this book is available
from the British Library.

ISBN 0 9533582 8 3

9 8 7 6 5 4 3 2 1

Dedicated as ever to every Thomas Lauredemmy everywhere.

ETHEL BARKING'S ENGLAND

AN AFFECTIONATE LOOK AT THE PAST 2000 YEARS OF THIS ISLAND'S GLORIOUS HISTORY

Foreword

by Doctor Ethel Barking B.A. (Lamb), B.Elch,
B.Onk, H.Onk, B.Sc. (Spitfire Renovation)

'Albion', 'Sceptred Isle', 'Britannia' - what glorious deeds these immortal names evoke, dear reader, as we look back over two thousand years of a proud nation's evolution from pre-Celtic herders to the House of Saxe Coburg and Harrods.

Did Caesar really get a good 'iding in Rome? Did Alfred the Grate really burn those cakes? Was Ethelred the Unready consistently impotent? Was 'Offa's Dyke' more likely a fragment from an ancient porn shop prosecution? More importantly, can Edward II justifiably lay claim to be our greatest Queen?

As the Visiting Professor in English History at King Ethelbert University, Reculver, Kent, it has fallen to me to adopt the mantle of putting the record straight. Of writing down once and for all the *real* England, the *real* reasons behind the myths of history, of sorting the wheat from the chaff, the winnow from the groin, the goose from the gander.

Read on, read on! Glory in your past, revere your present and, more importantly, look forward to a future where England (now that we are no longer to be held back by the shackles of our former Scottish and Welsh possessions) will rise once again to its former glory!

Viva Britannia!

Doctor Ethel Barking

THE FIRST
PEOPLE
c. 250,000 BC

The first acknowledged settlement of the British Isles occurred around 250,000 BC, when its land mass was still attached to Europe and you didn't have to fork out on exhorbitant ferry tickets. The fact that it separated from Europe in 6000 BC *(proving that even way back then, the people knew what they wanted. Ethel.)* thus creating the English Channel, has been forgotten by late 20th Century politicians who seem Canute-like *(see later, Ethel.)* in their determination to turn back the tide *(again, see later. Ethel.)*.

But of all the tribes who peopled this fair land way back then, the most important for our story are the Celts, a nomadic peoples from Eastern Europe and Asia who at one time ruled vast tracts of land from Turkey to Ireland.

THE ANCIENT BRITONS
c. 600 BC

Those Celts who settled in this fair island around 600 BC became known as Britons and their language is still with us today in the native tongues of Welsh, Cornish, Celtic, Irish and Gaelic, and many of their words are still here in place names. *(Eg Dover means Water - very clever, the Celts - and burgh means 'town', which is why you don't find many Burgher Kings in the countryside. Ethel.)*

The Britons were led by their Chiefs *('natch, Ethel.)* but their priests, called Druids, would often lead them into battle, all of them painted in blue wode (a clay-like substance) to make themselves look more fearsome to their foes. Women in this country had a hard and short life in those days, hence the public resistance then (and in some cases still today) to anything stamped 'Maid in Britain'.

"Ere, where did you learn your Wode Drill?"

THE ROMANS
55 BC

Then of course, came the Romans, the greatest empire builders of their day and keen to add to it. They already ruled all the lands around the Mediterranean and most of Western Europe up to the banks of the River Rhine. Romans reputedly got their name from the fact they roamed freely over most of the ancient world.

"Sorry I'm late; the *bloody* French closed the tunnel again!

By the time Caesar first visited in 55 BC, Britons were already making a meal of trading with Italy and its great trading cities - Pizza, Cannelone, Bolognese, etc. Julius Caesar was the greatest soldier of his time, and everywhere he went you would hear people calling out to him 'Hail, Caesar! Hail Caesar!' as a sign of the respect felt for him. Later, after he contracted asthma through spending too many Winters in damp old Britain, people changed their cry to 'Inhale Caesar! Inhale Caesar!' as he puffed away on his inhaler.

On his first visit, then, to see if invasion was feasible, Caesar landed near Deal on the Kent coast, fought a

Just a Roman in the gloamin

close-run battle with the native Brits, came to terms with the enemy *(the origin, in fact, of the term 'made a Deal'. Ethel.)* and went away peacefully.

However, now knowing that invasion was a distinct possibility, he returned in 54 BC in great numbers, subdued the local tribes and then left the country again very suddenly because of a crisis back in Rome. He never returned, as he was famously killed by his enemies on the Ides (15th) of March in 44 AD. *(It hardly needs stating that this is the origin of a 'bloody good 'iding'. Ethel.)*

The only notable phrase of Caesar's to have been handed down to us from this famous period of our history is his classic 'Weni, widi, wiwi' - 'I came, I saw, I wet myself'.

BOUDICCA, THE FIRST ESSEX GIRL 43 AD

Britain was then free of Romans until AD 43, when the new Emperor of Rome, Claudius, invaded for a third time and this time came to stay. But he didn't have it all his own way, though!

We only need to look at the story of Boadicea (Boudicca), Queen of the Iceni, who rebelled against the Roman occupation and roamed over Essex in souped-up chariots with sharp blades sticking out from the axles and fluffy mead jugs hanging from the whips. Her Escorts were similarly armed and were expert at attacking river crossing points (called Fords) protected by Roman soldiers from the Capri, Consul, Focus, Ka and Mondeo Legions.

Boudicca razed *(ie. flattened. The English language is so odd, think you not? Ethel.)* many Roman towns in 61

THE FIRST ESSEX GIRL TRYING HER FIRST SNAKEBITE

AD, including London and Colchester - the original Essex Girl. In fact she and her soldiers slaughtered 20,000 Romans before final defeat and death at her own hand with an asp to her bosom. Legend has it that she is now buried under platform 10 at King's Cross station in London, which is rather strange given that no trains from King's Cross went to Essex, even then.

ROMANS LEAVE OUR SHORES 407 AD

But we digress. The Romans, with their superior fighting tactics, eventually held all the country except those little bits on the side called Wales and Scotland and the country prospered under their rule for some three hundred years. As Offa later built a famous dyke along his border with Wales to keep out the Britons, so Hadrian built a huge wall to keep the Picts and Scots out of Roman Britain.

All good things must come to an end, however, and all Roman troops left Britain in 407AD to defend Rome, which by then was under increasing attacks from its enemies in the East. It was all to no avail, alas, as Rome fell anyway to Alaric's Vandal hordes in 410 AD. *(In fact it fell quite quickly - with Alaricrity, as some critics have suggested. Ethel.)*

ANGLES, SAXONS
AND JUTES
407 - 460 AD

There then followed a large period of instability. Saxons had already started making raids while the Romans were here, as had Vikings, hence the coastal defences set up by the Romans under the command of the grandly named 'Count of the Saxon Shore'. These defences soon fell into disuse after the Romans left.

Over the next forty years, tribes from Germany, the Netherlands and Scandinavia drifted over and colonised large parts of England. The Angles' land became Anglia, with the North Folk - Norfolk - at one end and the South Folk - Suffolk - at the other. *(Proving beyond doubt that the Angles were almost as creative with language as the Celts. Ethel.)*

"Of course I'm a good Count. Listen. One shore, two shores, sea shores, fourshores ..."

VORTIGERN OPENS THE THAMES BARRIER 470 AD

Then, in 470 AD, Vortigern, a King of the British so called because he couldn't stand heights *(ie he suffered from Vortigo, Ethel.)*, hired some Saxons from Jutland *(so called because it juts out into the sea between modern-day Germany and Scandinavia, Ethel.)* to come over and help protect his land. Landing in East Kent, these mercenaries were led by the brothers Hengist and Horsa *(who was killed later, so Horsa was no Morsa.*

HENGIST AND HORSA ARRIVE IN PEGWELL BAY ON THE DAILY BOVERCRAFT

Ethel.), who soon realised that Britain was ripe for the taking and sent word back for all their friends and their families to come and help themselves - which they did. Over the next 80 years or so, as the Saxon hordes became larger and larger, the Ancient Brits were slowly pushed further and further back Westwards, into Wales, Cornwall and across the channel to Brittany.

ARTHUR SAVES THE DAY
c. 550 AD

KING ARTHUR - MYTH OR REALITY?

Records are naturally scarce from this period, but it is true from literature of around that time that a British warrior won fame by beating the Saxons at two key battles and holding back their advance across Britain for at least 50 years. There are some theories that he was in fact a Romano-British General called Arturius but nobody knows for sure. The myths of Avalon and Lancelot and the Knights of the Round Table were started much later by authors such as Mallory who wrote his Le Morte D'Arthur while languishing in gaol around 1468, nearly a thousand years after the time of Arthur *(so a fat lot he'd have known then! Ethel.)*

But the Anglo Saxons didn't have it all their own way - far from it! A famous British leader emerged who held back the Saxon advance for a good 50 years *(a little known fact is Arthur's surname, which was in fact Century. Arthur Century, yes? 50 years? Geddit? Ethel.)* through two famous victories, one at Mount Badon and the second,

where he sadly died, at the Battle of Camlamn. No-one knows where these battles took place, but everyone knows the name of this hero - none other than King Arthur, he of the Knights of the Round Table, the Holy Grail and Queen Guinevere with Lancelot *(and we know how he got his name, don't we children? Ethel.)*

BRITAIN
BECOMES
ENGLAND
c. 600 AD

But by 600 AD the Anglo (English) Saxons all but ruled over all the land, and Britain was soon to be no more. King Offa of Mercia built a huge barrier along his borders with Wales to keep the British out (Offa's Dyke). Legend has it that King Accept of Wessex also built a similar but more wavy structure (Accept's Benda) along his borders with Cornwall to keep the Brits out but no trace remains of it.

OH, OH,
HERE THEY
COME AGAIN!

But even as the Anglo Saxons were settling down to their new possession, forming the great kingdoms of Wessex, Mercia and Northumbria among others, other invaders were already eyeing up England. Vikings *(actually Norwegians but coming from fjords, called viks in Norwegian, hence the name. Ethel.)* and Danes started serious raiding.

THE DANES
c. 870 AD

They came in ships called longboats, so called because they had a long way to go, and by 870 AD the Danish armies had conquered almost a third of the country, north of a line following the old Roman road Watling Street running North-West from

London to Chester. Alfred, King of Wessex in the other half of the country, paid the Danish army off with what was called Danegeld to stop them coming any further, and the land held by the Danes was afterwards called the Danelaw.

(A similar parallel can be drawn in the 20th Century. The Viking equivalent of that time - the Abba Hordes - levied their Danegeld in the form of worthless plastic discs that made horrible cat-like noises when scratched at speed. Ethel.)

ALFRED
THE GRATE
871 - 899

The Danes kept their promises for four years before starting attacking again and King Alfred had to go into hiding. There is a famous story of how the King got his name; on being told by a peasant woman to watch the cakes she was cooking in her cottage grate, he was berated by her when she returned home to find them burnt to a crisp. *(But then, what else can one expect of a man? Ethel.)*

After the burning shame of this minor setback, Alfred slowly regrouped his army, then took to the

"That really does take the biscuit. Doesn't she realise I'm King?"

field and severely beat the invaders in battle, finally capturing London in 886 AD.

After that peace reigned and Alfred eventually went from Alfred the Grate to Alfred the Great through all his good works. Under later Wessex Kings the whole country became peacefully unified between the English and the Danes. Further trouble then broke out when in the 980s raiders came over from Denmark again, this time under the rule of a very nasty piece of Scandinavian nativity called King Swein Forkbeard.

ETHEL BARKING'S
ENGLAND

END OF PART ONE

PART TWO

THE SECOND
THOUSAND YEARS

ETHELRED
(978-1016)
AND
CANUTE
(1016-1035)

Ethelred, a very weak King and known as the Unready *(presumably by his reputedly insatiable wife. Ethel.)*, paid a huge Danegeld to get Swein Forkbeard to leave but refused to meet his aggressor face to face under the pretence that 'Never the Swain shall meet'. This didn't stop Forkbeard from temporarily seizing the Kingdom in 1013, though *(the dirty double-crossing Swein, Ethel.)*.

But this peace didn't last long, and after Ethelred's death the Witan *(the early English Parliament, as opposed to today's Parliament called the Witless, Ethel.)* elected King Swein's younger son Cnut (Canute) to be King of all England as it seemed to them the best way to avoid paying more Danegeld was to become part of the Danish system!

Crowned in 1016, Cnut was a good king, and also became King of Denmark when his father died in 1019. Legend has it that he sat on the beach while the tide came in to prove to his councillors that he was not all-powerful and could not control the tide. *(A courtier from another Kingdom, asking for an audience, was told he would have to wait as the King was 'tide up and couldn't sea anyone'. Ethel.)*

When Cnut died in 1042, the Witan elected his son Edward, who was in fact Alfred's great-great-grandson, as Cnut had married Alfred's widow to show solidarity with the English when he took the throne *(typical bloody man! Ethel)*.

EDWARD THE CONFESSOR 1042-1066

This Edward was known as Edward the Confessor, because he was very naughty as a boy but always owned up, but when he died in 1066 there were no less than four claimants to the throne - Duke William of Normandy, Harold Hardrada of Norway, Harold Godwineson of Wessex (Harold Hardrada's brother in law) and Tostig Earl of Northumbria. Edward, however, having allegedly offered the throne to Duke William some years before, named Harold of Wessex as the new King on his deathbed, and after that all hell broke loose!

This is briefly what happened. Tostig fled across the North Sea to Norway to give allegiance to Harold Hardrada, while King Harold kept his army in the South and blockaded the Channel because he knew a very cross Duke William was amassing an army across the English Channel. Harald Hardrada then took advantage of this and invaded from the North, so King Harold had to hot foot it up there with his army to kill him and Tostig at the Battle of Stamford Bridge - Surrender? Nor-Way, pal!

(ENGLAND 1, NORWAY 0).

Historians argue that William of Normandy got his name William the Bastard because he was the illegitimate son of Robert, Duke of Normandy, but in reality it was because he was simply a thoroughly bad lot.

He was also French *(hey, nobody's perfect. Ethel.)*, and being French rather unsportingly chose Harald Hardrada's invasion in the North as the precise moment to invade in the South.

Harold thus had to force march his men down South again, met William at Senlac Hill near Hastings in 1066 and was roundly beaten and indeed slaughtered

(FRANCE 1, ENGLAND 0).

Experts now say that the soldier with the arrow in the eye was not King Harold, but a certain Saxon retainer *(surely that should be retailer? Ethel.)* called Captain Bird's Eye. We know this because this famous incident is frozen for all time in a scene from the Bayeux Tapestry.

NORMAN KINGS
1066-1154

WILLIAM I	1066-1087
WILLIAM RUFUS	1087-1100
HENRY I	1100-1135
STEPHEN	1135-1154

WILLIAM I
1066-1087

Even though William was crowned King on Christmas Day 1066, it took the Normans almost the rest of William's life to conquer the entire country, with the Domesday Book record of everything belonging to him in England being completed between 1084 and 1086.

WILLIAM RUFUS 1087-1100

William 1st died in 1087 after a very busy 21 years on the throne and was succeeded by his brother Rufus as William II, who only ruled for three years before being killed in a hunting accident in the New Forest. *(Probably during a stag party. Ethel.)*

And that's when the problems started all over again!

THE TOWER OF LONDON

William built new timber walling onto the existing Roman fortifications to keep the people of London in check, but over the centuries this magnificent castle has been added to and added to as it has served as fortress, as a palace - in fact the key residence for all English Kings from William II right through to Henry VII - a prison and place of execution, and the home of the Crown Jewels. *(Some tourists, particularly raunchy women, come to London in the belief that the Tower of London and Big Ben are <u>not</u> buildings. I don't know why. Ethel.)*

HENRY I
1100 - 1135

You see, William's line ruled by force of arms, the crown being passed from one strong father to strong son and so on. Thus Henry 1st succeeded William Rufus, but Henry 1st's son William died young and so the crown should have passed to Henry's daughter Matilda as next in line when Henry Ist popped his clogs.

Whoops!

STEPHEN (1135-1154)
AND MATILDA

For the next 20 years England was plunged into uncivil war *(although the history books call it a Civil War. Ethel.)* between Matilda and Stephen, Henry's nephew.

THE HEIRLESS KING STEPHEN.

A lot of the Barons did not like the idea of being ruled by a woman *(personally I see absolutely no problem with a woman as ruler. Ethel.)* and Henry 1st's nephew, Stephen, had stolen the crown soon after Henry's death. With no-one in effective charge of the country, the Barons roamed and plundered at will and became very powerful. At long last, however, Stephen died and left no heir to follow him, paving the way for Matilda's son Henry of Anjou to come over from France and take over *(another blasted frog hopping across the Channel! Ethel.)*

THE PLANTAGENETS
1154-1399

HENRY II	1154-1189
RICHARD	1189-1199
JOHN	1199-1216
HENRY III	1216-1272
EDWARD I	1272-1307
EDWARD II	1307-1377
RICHARD II	1377-1399

HENRY II
1154-1189

Henry II's surname was Plantagenet, named after the Latin words for the yellow bloom flowers *(planta genista, or the broom)* that made up his father's heraldic emblem. *(See other horticultural conflicts later in this volume, viz. The 15th Century Wars of the Roses, the 20th Century Wars of the Garden Centres, and of course Weed Wars I and II. Ethel.)*

By adding England to his empire he became the most powerful King in Europe, his marriage to Eleanor of Aquitaine already having more than doubled the lands he controlled.

THE NEW BROOMS SWEEP CLEAN

Henry II swiftly set about putting the too-powerful Barons in their place. He had over three hundred illegally-built castles burned down *(He allegedly sent a message to each of these Barons, saying simply 'Come home to a real fire'. Ethel.)* and then set about gaining control of the armed forces. Until then, the Barons were charged with supplying the King with armed soldiers (Knights) in times of war, but all too often they had been used by the Barons for their own ends during the week (Days).

Henry introduced a special tax called 'scutage' (shield money) which the Barons paid to the King instead of providing him with troops. The King used this money to pay his own soldiers and so developed the first professional army and weakened the power of the Barons at the same time.

But apart from being a strong soldier, he is also credited with having started our current system of law, developing a 'Common Law' that was the same throughout the land and appointing judges to travel around the country holding cases at regular assizes. *(For more information on the development of the law under his successor, Richard, see my Ph.D. thesis "King Dick: Assize too big to handle". Ethel.)*

But this very attempt to introduce a more just society backfired with a vengeance. At that time churchmen were incredibly powerful people and had the right to be tried in their own church courts, where punishments were far less harsh. Wanting to change this, Henry II made his good friend Thomas à Becket the new Archbishop of Canterbury to help get church support, but once he was appointed Becket took the church's side and openly defied the King.

Silly billy! *(That's the trouble with Bishoprics: they always have to be kept in hand. Ethel.)*

In desperation at this turn of events, Henry II flew into a furious rage and shouted out: "Will not someone rid me of this turbulent priest?" Unfortunately he was heard by four of his Knights, who taking him at his word then took themselves swiftly off to Canterbury Cathedral and turned Becket into an instant martyr by the carefree application of sword blades sharp and various.

"Phew! Bit turbulent today Thomas."

RICHARD
LIONHEART
1189-1199

Well what a King he was! Thought of as a hero for centuries, what is the reality? Of a ten-year reign, he only spent seven months in England, preferring the sands of the Holy Land to fight in the Crusades to return Jerusalem to Christian influence rather than leave it in the hands of his arch enemy Saladin. Captured on his way home, he cost his people a fortune in ransoms, and he even pardoned the archer who fired the arrow that killed him in 1199. *(How could he pardon someone if he were dead? Ethel.)*

KING JOHN
1199-1216

John of course, Richard's brother, has been vilified over the years as the man who tried to kill Robin Hood, but history now shows him in a slightly better light. True, he lost most of England's French possessions. True, he fell out with the Pope. True, he lost his war chest and jewels in the Wash. True, he upset people with high levels of taxation, and true, he <u>was</u> forced to sign the Magna Carta. *(Okay, so he wasn't all that good. Next! Ethel.)*

MAGNA CARTA

King John signed the Magna Carta (the Great Deed) on June 15th 1215, in a meadow at Runnymede *(it was formerly a brewery for weak cider. Ethel)*. It was an attempt by the Barons to curb the King's powers. It was a hugely significant document in the history of England. The Pope, however, decreed that King John need not adhere to the Charter, which led to Civil War that only ended with John's death. *(If you refer back to the entry for Vortigern, you will see that, as usual, the Horsa did indeed come before the Carta. Ethel.)*

Magna Carta (Latin for 'A huge truck')

"YOU DUMP WE HUMP"

MAGNA CARTS Co.

PSS

HENRY III
1216-1272

Only nine when he came to the throne at John's death, Henry III had two Regents appointed, and with them he ruled wisely. Then, in 1227, he took over personally, and everything went downhill from there. First he married a Frenchwoman, Eleanor of Provence *(asking for trouble! Ethel.)*, and then appointed a series of French advisers to help him rule England! Not on, said the Barons, and another civil war broke out. In 1265, one of the Barons, Simon de Montfort, summoned the first English Parliament, but the Barons fell out and eventually de Montfort (who was incidentally Henry's brother-in-law) was killed in battle by forces led by Henry's son and successor, Edward. *(To all intents and purposes then, de Montfort's nephew. Some family! Mind you, he did have a French mother-in-law. Ethel.)*

"Richard, John,
Henry Three,

But I'm the one
who built
Salisbury!"

EDWARD I
1272-1307

Edward I is best known for his attempts to unite Scotland with England, which he accomplished in 1292 when he appointed one John Balliol to be King when the rightful heir Margaret, Maid of Norway, died on her way home to claim the crown. Later, when Edward summonsed Balliol to accompany him on a campaign in France, he refused, so Edward invaded Scotland, deposed Balliol *(who, apart from that, got off Scot-free. Ethel)* and took over the throne himself. He also removed the Stone of Scone, the seat of the throne *(and the first recorded Rock Cake. Ethel)* to Westminster.

He also, in that friendly and neighbourly way of his, invaded Wales, adding it to the Kingdom in 1292. But the Scots were not to be so lightly dismissed, rebelling under their leader William Wallace and thrashing Edward at the Battle of Stirling Bridge. Edward then thrashed Wallace at Falkirk, and Wallace was eventually betrayed and executed in London, bearing a more than passing resemblance to that great Australian actor whose name escapes the author.

Another thing for which Edward is famous is creating the very first Prints of Wales (*every one with a Snowdonia background. Colour £3.50, black and white £2 from the castle gift shop. Ethel*), a tradition still in use today for the Monarch's eldest son.

Edward was called 'Longshanks'. Because they were.

EDWARD II
1307-1327
England's greatest Queen?

Edward II is probably our saddest Queen (sorry, King) *ever*. Brought up in a household full of women (*nothing wrong with that. Ethel.*) and with his father absent for long periods, perhaps it's no wonder he grew up a bit confused about mummies and daddies.

Whatever the reasons, and despite the fact he married Isabella of France (*grrrrrrr! Ethel*) in 1308 and produced four children, it is a well documented fact that he batted for the other side. His many lovers (sorry, advisers) included Piers Gaveston - killed by the King's opponents in 1312 - and later Sir Hugh Despenser and his son Hugh. He also

famously lost the Battle of Bannockburn in 1314 at the hands of Robert the Bruce, thus guaranteeing Scotland's independence. But that's by the by.

ROBERT THE BRUCE BEFORE THE BATTLE OF BANNOCKBURN 1314. THE FIRST KNOWN USE OF THE WEB FOR INSPIRATION.

Isabella, humiliated and probably left wanting in the old horizontal heave-ho department by her errant husband, took Roger Mortimer as her lover and together they plotted the King's overthrow. This they achieved in 1327, with the Despensers being executed *(the origin of the phrase 'to be Despensed with'. Ethel.)* and Edward being locked up in Berkeley Castle. There he was brutally murdered on Isabella's and Mortimer's orders, *(but not in a very nice way, dear children. Ethel.)* In those days, the conventional way of executing those of another persuasion was to disembowel them by inserting a red-hot poker into the aforementioned errant bottom. Isabella wanted no marks on the body, however, as she wanted it to be known he had died of natural causes, so in Edward's case the poker was inserted through a hunting horn to leave no trace. The fact his screams could be heard from one end of the land to the other apparently hadn't occurred to her. *(So from Bannockburn to Bottomburn in just 13 years, eh? Ethel.)*

EDWARD III
1327-1377

After Edward II's gruesome murder, Isabella and Mortimer didn't have it all their own way. After ruling for the next three years in the name of the young Edward III, this latter suddenly assumed the reigns of power, had Mortimer's head removed rather swiftly and banished his own mother from public life. *(And he was only 17 at the time. Ungrateful boy! Ethel.)*

THE FRENCH FLEE THE BATTLEFIELD.
BATTLE OF CRECY 1346.

THE TWO-FINGERED GESTURE

Everyone knows the two-fingered gesture is generally made as a sign of bravado and disdain by lads the world over, but its origins are apparently from the English archers before Crécy, or even earlier. English archers were feared throughout Europe and if captured their enemies would cut off their two bow-drawing fingers. So, before the battle, and after it, when the English had annihilated the cream of French nobility *(what's that, a soup? Ethel.)* they all waved their two fingers in the air to show they had won the day.

Edward III famously started a very long fight with the French, called The Hundred Years War *(so called because it lasted from 1337 to 1453 and arithmetic was not then a compulsory subject at school. Ethel.)* His son, the Black Prince, achieved fame on the battlefields of Crécy in 1346 and at Poitiers in 1356, but sadly died of a wasting disease in Spain a year before his father. *(A bit of a wastral, then? Ethel.)*

Edward II also made English the official language in Parliament and the courts instead of French, so you could say he made up for a lot of his shortcomings with just that one act!

"At last! Let's celebrate with a bottle of Cabernet Sauvignon!"

RICHARD II
1377-1399

Richard II *(the second in a series of rulers who have proved just what happens when you have too many dicks running things. Ethel.)* was the grandson of Edward III, the son of the Black Prince *(although Richard himself was white. Ethel.)* and was only 10 when he came to the throne. For a while advisers, including his Uncle, John of Gaunt, ruled in his name, but Richard soon got rid of them and while he was at it exiled John of Gaunt's son, Henry Bolingbroke, who also had claim to the throne. He was actually quite a wise King until his wife died, after which he became a complete and utter mumbling loony and needed replacing.

When John of Gaunt died, Henry Bolingbroke became Duke of Lancaster and deposed Richard in 1399 to become our very own Henry IV, the first in a long line of Lancastrian Kings.

The Peasants' Revolt 1381

The call 'The peasants are revolting' has reverberated down history, and in general it is true to say they are. Richard III's particular little skirmish with the working classes came when the peasants rebelled against both low wages and a new poll tax that charged everyone the same amount irrespective of how much money they had. On the way to London the peasants killed the Archbishop of Canterbury and the King's treasurer, but were stopped at Smithfield in London *(after all, a meat market is an obvious place to meet, n'est-ce pas? Ethel.)* where the Lord Mayor killed one of the leaders, Wat Tyler, and the King made false promises to get the rioters to disperse. *(Along with Wat Tyler, most of the other ringleaders, including Which Roofer, Why Doubleglaze and Wherefor Closet, were also caught and hanged. Ethel.)*

Geoffrey Chaucer

The poet wrote his famous yet inutterably incomprehensible-to-millions Canterbury Tales between 1387 and 1398 in very dodgy English. It has since become an international best-seller.

THE HOUSE OF LANCASTER 1399-1461

HENRY IV	1399-1413
HENRY V	1413-1422
HENRY VI	1422-1461,
	Half-time
	1470 - 1471

HENRY IV 1399-1413

To be perfectly blunt, Henry IV spent most of his time being revolting in Wales. Owain Glendower, a descendent of the ancient Welsh princes, is held largely to blame, *(but then boyos will be boyos, will they not? Ethel.)*, as he was being equally revolting in his attempts to make Wales independent. *(Even to the extent of inviting a French army over to help him! Unforgivable. Ethel.)* In fact Henry spent a lot of his reign in fighting off dissent from his subjects, including three rebellions by his arch rivals, the Percy family.

The result of all this pressure? All this warring wore poor old Henry out. He died in 1413 and was replaced by his son.

HENRY V
1413-1422

Henry V, of course, was a totally different kettle of
fish. He plumped straight back into war with
France, and before you could say Harry and St
George or similar he wupped them at a little place
called Agincourt on October 25th 1415. A major
victory, but not such a big bag as at Crécy nearly a
century before.

FRANCE THRASHED
6000 - 400.

ENGLAND
KEEPS CUP!

AGINCOURT
ENGLAND **1** - FRANCE LOST

There the French lost 10,000 men to England's 200. At Agincourt, only 6,000 Frenchmen for the loss of 400 Englishmen. *(Well Brian, the lads have had two key fixtures in the space of 69 years, and it's not even the end of the season yet. They're a bit tired, a bit under pressure, and I'm a little concerned about the back four, but I'm sure the return matches will see us back on top form. Ethel.)*

Henry also managed to wangle an agreement from the French King Charles VI to appoint him his heir upon marriage to Charles' daughter Catherine. Sadly both Henry and Charles died before this could come about, so he ended up King of absolutely nothing.

HENRY VI
1422-1461,
(half time)
1470-1471

Basically, Henry VI was a nutter. Not only did he lose all England's French possessions, not only did he go loopy to such an extent that he had to have a substitute halfway through his reign. Those two things alone would have guaranteed him a place in history - but to be thrashed by a woman as well?! *(Oi! Ethel.)*

"Votre Bifsteak, madamoiselle. Bleu ou bien cui?

THE WARS OF THE ROSES
1455 - 1485

There's usually one side of the family you don't talk to. Uncle Bert who did something dodgy with nylons during the war; Rosy who was no better than she ought to be when the Fleet was in; Cousin Kevin who we don't talk about in polite company, dear! The Wars of the Roses was that sort of family feud, but on a slightly bigger scale between the Royal Houses of Lancaster and York and raging all over the country instead of all over the kitchen. The Yorkists got fed up with Henry VI's weak rule, the Lancastrians got fed up with the Yorks getting fed up with Henry VI's weak rule, and so it went on. Up and down the country they raged, a battle here, a skirmish there, until eventually one Henry Tudor, a Lancastrian, beat the whoopsy out of Edward IV's brother Richard III at the Battle of Bosworth Field and got himself crowned King of England as Henry VII. *(Recent research by the Whitechapel Branch of the Ladies of a Certain Persuasion Society has suggested the Wars of the Roses were so named because of the large number of pricks to be found on both sides. Ethel. Or was it thorns?)*

The woman in question was, of course, Joan of Arc, a peasant girl from Eastern France who had a vision telling her to drive the hated English out of France. This vision led to a French revolt that resulted in the English indeed being driven out of all their French possessions except Calais by 1453. Joan herself was captured by the English in 1431 and burned at the stake in the French town of Rouen. *(I have written extensively elsewhere of the events that eventually led to her Rouen. Ethel.)*

But Henry VI's mind went, poor love, and he was forced to appoint a Protector, Richard Duke of York, while he got his act back together. In 1455, however, Richard was dismissed and rebelled against the King, which was the start of the Wars of the Roses. Henry was then deposed by Richard the Protector's son, Edward, who then had himself crowned Edward IV. Henry wangled his throne back for a brief spell in 1470, but then was subsequently murdered in the Tower of London.

All round, a bit of a saddy.

THE HOUSE OF YORK 1461-1485

EDWARD IV	1461-1470, 1471-1483
HENRY VI	1470-1471
EDWARD IV	1471-1483
EDWARD V	1483
RICHARD III	1483-1485

EDWARD IV 1461-1470, 1471-1483

Already largely covered in the sad and weepy story of Henry VI, Edward IV ruled twice, and is really most famous for allegedly having his brother George, Duke of Clarence, murdered in the Tower of London in a butt of malmsey wine. *(Apparently for taking the piss out of him. Ethel.)*

Edward had a bit of a rocky ride, really, having come to the throne when only 19 after defeating Henry VI and being proclaimed King by his cousin Warwick 'The Kingmaker'. He fell out with Warwick, who then joined Henry VI's wife Margaret in a rebellion.

Warwick was killed by Edward IV at the Battle of Barnet in 1471 *(see also the Battles of Hairpiece, Toupé and Wig later that same year. Ethel.)* Another key fact learned by generations of eager schoolchildren is that William Caxton, the famous printer, set up shop in Edward's reign, in Westminster in 1476.

EDWARD V
1483

This is the sad story of The Princes in the Tower. Edward V was the 13 year-old son of Edward IV, who in his will appointed his brother Richard Duke of Gloucester to be Protector until Edward V came of age. But naughty Richard didn't fancy the idea of having to give the crown away, so had Edward and his younger brother Richard declared illegitimate *(the bastard! Ethel)* and had them locked in the Tower of London. They were never seen again, and no-one to this day can say with any certainty what happened to them. *(So from Caxton's prints in Westminster to no Prince in the Tower eh? Pretty damn rum, I call it. Ethel.)*

As there were surprisingly no other candidates, William of Gloucester became William III and took the throne in 1483.

RICHARD III
1483-1485

The man who let in the Tudors and the last Yorkist King, Richard III has been vilified over the years, not least by Shakespeare, who portrayed him as a hunchback.

It is now generally thought that he wasn't such a bad King after all, but then there's not a lot you can really do wrong when you're only on the throne for two years, now is there? *(Mind you, you know what they say: to mislay one nephew could be called careless. To mislay two nephews, well ..... Ethel.)*

But Richard III got his cumuppence, and came to a very sticky end after Henry Tudor landed in Wales and brought an army of 8,000 men to face Richard's 12,000 men at the Battle of Bosworth on the 22 August 1485. Legend has it that William was wearing his crown when he was struck down, and it rolled under a bush, from where it was retrieved by Lord Stanley and placed on Henry's head. *(Well, let's just hope it was a Rose bush, dear children! Ethel.)*

THE TUDORS
1485-1603

HENRY VII	1485-1509
HENRY VIII	1509-1547
EDWARD VI	1547-1553
MARY I	1553-1558
ELIZABETH I	1558-1603

HENRY VII
1485 - 1509

Henry Tudor (or more accurately in its Welsh form, Tudur) claimed a right to the throne through being the great-great grandson of John of Gaunt *(see earlier. Ethel.)*. Once King, Henry married Elizabeth of York, Edward IV's daughter, and thus united the Houses of York and Lancaster into the new House of Tudor and brought peace to the country.

In general his reign remained peaceful, marred only slightly by two claimants to the throne: Lambert Simnel in 1487 and Perkin Warbeck in 1492, both disposed of in a time-honoured fashion. He also invaded France *(excellent. Ethel.)* and withdrew on payment of a large sum of money *(even better. Ethel,)*. Henry died at Richmond Palace in 1509 and is generally thought of as a good egg.

THE AGE OF AMERICAN EXPLORATION

This was the start of the age of the great explorers. Christopher Columbus discovered America in 1492 *(although there are claims that the Vikings found it first, but didn't like the way they were portrayed by Burt Lancaster in the Hollywood film of that name, so didn't stay. Ethel)* and Henry himself sponsored the voyages of the Cabot brothers to North America in 1497. A hundred years later Sir Walter Raleigh made his first voyage to South America, and of course in 1620 the Pilgrim Fathers made their famous voyage to America in the Mayflower *(and celebrated their first Mass in a place called Chussets. Ethel)*. Francis Drake, of course, made his round-the-world voyage in 1577-1580 and managed to miss America altogether! *(This event is celebrated every year in the Miss America Contest. Ethel.)*

HENRY VIII
1509 - 1547

We all know about Henry and his six wives, two of whom he had executed. His first marriage, in 1509, was in fact to his widowed sister-in-law, Catherine of Aragon. He didn't like her much and the marriage was annulled in 1533 *(wed 1509, fled 1533)*. Then came Anne Boleyn *(wed 1533, head 1536)*, Jane Seymour *(wed 1536, dead 1537)*, Anne of Cleves *(wed 1540, shed 1540)*, Catherine Howard *(wed 1540, head 1542)*, Catherine Parr *(wed 1543, widowed 1547)*.

(I have absolutely no comment to make on the fickleness of this man. Ethel. Perhaps he misunderstood sex-appeal for six-appeal?)

From a slim well-proportioned youth coming to the throne at 18 to a fat, gout- and pox-ridden maniac took Henry 37 years, the same amount of time it took him to have well over 50,000 people executed for various offences, least of which was not agreeing with his break with Rome and the hounding of Catholics (he had himself made Head of the Church of England in 1534). He is also famous for his Dissolution of the Monasteries, a very good and rewarding fund-raising initiative that got rid of hotbeds of Catholic dissent in the country as an additional benefit.

On the musical front Henry VIII is credited as the author of that very pleasant little ditty 'Greensleeves'. *(It goes without saying, of course, that Henry was very accomplished on the organ. Ethel.)* On the diplomatic front his summit meeting with King Francis I of France, at the Field of the Cloth of

"Weee! It's just like flying!"

A TITANIC MOMENT ON THE MAIDEN
VOYAGE OF HENRY'S FLAGSHIP

Gold in 1520, did little to stop the two countries continuing to bash each other's brains out over the passing years. *(The later meeting between the British and French Prime Ministers at a picnic in Windsor Great Park some 450 years later in 1970 is known rather less grandly as the Lawn of the Table Cloth from Marks & Sparks. Ethel.)*

THE REFORMATION

Martin Luther started it in 1517 with his publications attacking corruption in the Roman Catholic Church. Those who agreed with him broke away to become Protestants. Henry VIII supported the Catholic Church originally, but turned against it and declared himself Supreme Head of the Church of England when the Pope refused to let him divorce his first wife. *(Petulance! Ethel.)* Henry was excommunicated by the Pope in 1533. Henry's Lord Chancellor bore the brunt of this upheaval, but refused to acknowledge Henry as Head of the English Church, for which he was executed *(obviously a head of his time. Ethel).* His successor, Thomas Cromwell having successfully stripped the monasteries of their wealth during the Dissolution, was similarly executed for treason. 1535 saw the first English-language Bible.

Henry VIII will always be remembered as the ultimate six-pack.

EDWARD VI
1547-1553

Henry's son by Jane Seymour, Edward VI, came to the throne at the age of nine, but ruled throughout his six-year reign through two Protectors *(the first of whom, the Duke of Somerset, was killed off by his successor, the Earl of Warwick, in an early form of Protector Racket. Ethel.).* During this time the Reformation was much strengthened, with the Catholic Mass being declared illegal and a new Book of Common Prayer introduced. Sadly, Edward caught tuberculosis and snuffed it in 1553. *(Hence giving rise to one of Shakespeare's greatest lines: 'TB or not TB? That is the question." Ethel.)*

MARY I
1553-1558

To ensure a Protestant succession, Edward VI had nominated his niece Lady Jane Grey as Queen, but Mary, daughter of Henry VIII and Catherine of Aragon, had other ideas! A devout Catholic, she advanced on London, seized the throne and then started reintroducing Catholicism in a big big way. She topped Lady Jane Grey in 1554, burnt three

Protestant Bishops at the stake in 1555 and Thomas Cranmer, former Archbishop of Canterbury, was similarly reduced to ashes in 1556, with thousands more suffering torture and death at her hands as she rid the whole country of Protestant support *(the first Protest Movement? Ethel.)*

She also attacked France *(good on'ya! Ethel)* but got wupped and luckily managed to lose Calais, our very last French possession. Mary died in 1558 and her infamy lives on to this day in that well-known vodka-based drink. *(What on earth's a vodka martini got to do with the Reformation? Ethel.)*

ELIZABETH I
1558-1603

After Edward II, she was probably our best-loved Queen. Elizabeth put England on the world map and opened up a new world of exploration and achievement.

The daughter of Henry VIII and Anne Boleyn, she had herself appointed Head of the Church of England, but also cleverly appointed an Archbishop of Canterbury - Matthew Parker - who helped

"Yes please, Walt.
Bring me back a
Big Mac and a
large portion of
fried potatoes."

THE SPANISH ARMADA

Basically, if Philip of Spain hadn't tried to insist Lizzy I went back to Catholicism, all this wouldn't have happened. She also sent aid to the Dutch Protestants in Holland, at that time ruled by Spain, which didn't help much. The execution of Mary Queen of Scots was the final straw, and Philip ordered the Armada to invade England.

130 Spanish ships in all set sail from Lisbon, manned by 10,000 crew and with 20,000 soldiers on board. English ships fought the Armada all the way up the Channel until it anchored off Calais. *(Bloody Calais again. Ethel.)* Drake then sent in his fire ships, which panicked the Armada into cutting anchors and sailing away in confusion. *(An anagram of the word 'Armada' is, of course, 'Ram aad'. Ethel.)* After a heavy engagement with the English fleet they escaped up the East coast of England, round the top of Scotland and then down the West coast of Ireland, where many ships were lost in fierce storms. *(The dark complexion of many Irish people from those parts shows exactly what happened when the shipwrecked soldiers and sailors waded ashore. Absolutely disgraceful behaviour! Ethel.)*

In all, it is estimated that the Armada lost 11,000 men, a third of its strength.

create a more moderate environment in which both faiths could live side by side. In 1562 Hawkins and Drake made the first slave-trading trips to America, in 1577-80 Drake sailed around the world and Sir Walter Raleigh made his first expedition to South America in 1595. It wasn't all good news though. There was the little matter of Mary Queen of Scots, who fled to England after being thrown out of Scotland, only to be imprisoned and then beheaded by Elizabeth in 1587 *(an early incident of 'headed off at the border'. Ethel.)*. And of course the matter of the Armada in 1588, where Drake was famously interrupted playing bowls. *(Recent research suggests he was doing no such thing. Instead he was toying with a lady, and when being told of the fleet's sighting, remarked 'Oh balls. Alright, I'll be along in a minute.' Ethel.)*

On the arts' side, Edmund Spenser published his famous 'Faerie Queen' *(probably devoted to Edward II. Ethel)* in 1590 and Shakespeare gave the first performance of 'Hamlet' in 1601.

Elizabeth never married, of course, nor produced a successor. *(It is believed, however, that she greeted certain of her courtiers - Robert Dudley, Earl of Leicester, and his step-son The Earl of Essex, in particular - in a more, shall we say horizontal?, position than others. Ethel.)* Elizabeth I was the last of the Tudors. All in all, a jolly good reign for a bird.

STUARTS
1603-1714

JAMES I	1603-1625
CHARLES I	1625-1649
CHARLES II	1660-1685
JAMES II	1685-1688
WILLIAM III	1688-1702
(With MARY, died 1694)	
ANNE	1702-1714

As their were no more Tudors, Elizabeth I's heir was in fact the existing James VI of Scotland, who was the great grandson of Henry VIII's sister, Margaret Tudor. James' name had been changed to Stewart from the time his ancestors had been made hereditary Stewards of Scotland, the name being changed to the French version *(aaaaaaag! Ethel.)* of Stuart. James VI of Scotland thus also became James I of England, the first Stuart King of England.

JAMES I
1603-1625

By all accounts, James I was fat, vain, conceited and stupid, and had a tongue too large for his mouth. *(So how come their was so much room for him to put his foot in it so often? Ethel.)* He also believed in the Scottish view of Kingship - the Divine Right of Kings who had been appointed by God and therefore owed nothing to the common people *(a typical man, then. Ethel.)* which didn't make him all that many friends.

He did, however, manage to arrange peace with Spain, and his reign saw the flowering of Shakespeare *(yes, and the de-flowering of Anne Hathaway, too! Ethel.)* and the execution of Sir Walter Raleigh for treason in 1618. Probably the most famous event of his reign, The Gunpowder Plot of 1605, involving Guy (originally Guido) Fawkes, was an attempt by dissident Catholics to make the King more tolerant to their religion, but all it did was start up the worldwide multi-billion dollar firework industry! *(A little known fact is that Guido's brother, Lego Fawkes, fled to Scandinavia to escape persecution over the affair and started up another worldwide multi-million dollar toy business based on interlocking plastic shapes. Ethel.)*

Another multi-billion dollar worldwide industry

THE GUNPOWDER PLOT 1605

It was planned by Sir Robert Gatesby, a Catholic disappointed in the King's failure to grant Catholics more tolerance. He recruited a band of like-minded Catholics to blow up Parliament and the King. To this end, they dug a tunnel into a cellar under the House of Lords and filled it with gunpowder. One of the conspirators then got cold feet and shopped the lot of them. Guy Fawkes was found in the cellar ready to light the fuse and was tortured until he confessed all the names involved. They were all hung, drawn and quartered. *(This is a delicate operation involving hanging until nearly dead, then removing the intestines while still alive, and then rending the body apart into four quarters by the judicious use of ropes attached to each limb, and in turn attached to four horses galloping away in opposite directions. This not unusually results in the participant's death. Ethel.)* The Gunpowder Plot is celebrated each year on November 5th by burning an effigy of Guy Fawkes on a bonfire.

James I tried to *stop* was smoking, writing an impassioned plea called 'Counterblaste to Tobacco' *(hence leading to speculation in some quarters that he was in fact a fag. Ethel.)*. In his reign, too, the north of Ireland was colonised by Protestant settlers from England and Scotland after the Earls of Tyrone and Tyconnel ended their rebellion against the Crown. Fat, misshapen and Scottish: all in all, a bit of a haggis of a King.

CHARLES I
1625-1649

Chiefly remembered as the King who lost his head, Charles wouldn't have been King if his careless elder brother Henry hadn't popped his clogs in 1612. Charles inherited his father's idea of the Divine Right of Kings and was constantly quarrelling with Parliament, at one time ruling without it for 11 years because, as King, *he knew best*.

In 1628 his subjects came up with The Petition of Rights, and Charles agreed to it under protest, only to dissolve Parliament a year later and rule very autocratically until 1640. Then, he summonsed the Short Parliament *(even though it was held in the same-sized room as before. Ethel.)*, which lasted all of three weeks, then the Long Parliament *(see earlier comment. Ethel)* which lasted until 1660. By that time, of course, in 1649 to be precise, Parliament had had enough of both Charles *and* the Civil War he had caused, and chopped his head off. *(A very short King, he was found to be even shorter after this momentous event. Ethel.)*

The execution of Charles I opened the way for The Commonwealth, 1649-1660, the only time in the past thousand years when England has not been ruled over by a Monarch.

THE ENGLISH CIVIL WAR 1642-1649

Who was to rule England - the King or Parliament? That was the key cause of the Civil War, and it ended in defeat for the Royalist forces of Charles I, and victory for the Parliamentary forces under Oliver Cromwell.

Until 1644 the Royalists had it virtually all their own way, but defeat at Marston Moor in that year turned the tide, and Cromwell's New Model Army created by Parliament in 1645 crushed Royalist forces at the Battle of Naseby that same year. In 1646 Charles surrendered to the Scots, who promptly handed him over! Charles then conspired with the Scots to invade England, which led to defeat of a Scottish Army at Preston in 1648, followed by the trail and execution of the King on 30th January 1649. *(Students of phrase and fable should note that the origin of the phrase 'getting off Scot-free' obviously does not stem from this sad episode. Ethel.)*

The Royalist forces were called Cavaliers because of the loose wide-brimmed flowing hats they wore, reminiscent of the French Cavaliers. The Parliamentary soldiers were called Roundheads because of the round steel helmets they wore. *(Young boys often ask each other in the school playground whether they are Cavalier or Roundhead. I do not understand the reason for this strange question, or why they then go off in small groups and huddle behind the bike shed. Ethel.)*

THE COMMONWEALTH 1649-1660

The Commonwealth really had two parts. The Commonwealth proper from 1649 to 1653 was Cromwell trying to rule through the institution of Parliament, who disagreed with him so he disbanded it *(now where have we heard that one before, eh? Ethel.)* and the Protectorate from 1653 to 1659 was Cromwell ruling as Monarch in all but name, to be followed by his son Richard.

Cromwell, who died in 1658, is universally held to have been 'a good man', and during his years at the helm of state England's reputation across Europe went from strength to strength. The first Dutch War of 1652-4 saw the Dutch well and truly wupped, and Jamaica was captured from the Spanish in 1665. *(A very rum do indeed. Ethel.)*

A new Parliament was called in 1660 and negotiated the restoration of the monarchy under Charles II.

CHARLES II
1660-1685

Charles II had a very good life, largely devoted to his own pleasures. On taking over the crown, he was a popular King. Key events of his reign included the second and third Dutch Wars. *(These attractive girls all work in the red light district in Amsterdam, and all seem to have the surname Guilder. Hence, whenever you ask them what they are called, they answer Five Guilder, Fifty Guilder, etc. Ethel. Sorry, was that wars or whores?)*

His reign was also highlighted by the London Plague in 1665, which killed 100,000 Londoners in three months, and the Great Fire of London in 1666 which helped stop the disease spreading.

John Milton wrote Paradise Lost, John Bunyon knocked out his Pilgrim's Progress, Pepys started his diaries *(thus giving us an eye-witness peep at the London of that time. Ethel.)* work started on St. Paul's Cathedral and the Greenwich Observatory. The Test Act of 1673 banned Roman Catholics from playing cricket for England, and as a consequence in 1678 a man called Titus Oates reckoned to have uncovered a Popist plot to kill the King. He was hailed a hero in Charles' reign, but was accused of making the whole thing up and reviled in the reign of his successor.

Although married for well over 30 years, Charles kept at least one mistress on the go all the time *(once a King, always a King, once a Knight is <u>not</u> enough, then! Ethel.)* including the very famous Nell Gwynne, who allegedly kept oranges warm by sticking them up her jumper.

JAMES II
1685-1688

The younger brother of Charles II, James II returned to England at the Restoration and was made Lord High Admiral *(well, my dear, the <u>smell</u> after all those months at sea! Ethel.)* When he came to the throne, he made clear that he intended England to become Catholic again, but Monmouth's Rebellion of 1685 had to put everything else on hold. Monmouth was the illegitimate son of Charles II, and wanted to be King. James II didn't want him to be King, so met him in battle at Sedgmoor, thrashed him and executed him. End of rebellion.

THE GLORIOUS REVOLUTION

William was invited to 'rescue the nation and the religion' of England from the Catholicism of James II because first, he was a Protestant and second, and rather handily, was also married to James' eldest daughter Mary. He left his base in the Netherlands, landed at Brixham in Devon and started his long march to London. Along the way he was joined by thousand upon thousand of the common people. In less than two months he was in London and James was in exile. When the dust had settled, Parliament agreed to settle the crown jointly on William and Mary *(must have been a pretty funny-shaped crown. Ethel.)*. The Bill of Rights of 1689 established that no Catholic could become Monarch *(which is why you don't see many 'Pope for King' posters about these days. Ethel.)* and that taxes could not be raised or laws dispensed with without the permission of Parliament.

The birth of a son by his Catholic wife Princess Mary of Modena *(not to be confused with Dorothy of*

Doncaster or Bertha of Birmingham. Ethel.) caused so much conflict with Parliament that leading statesmen invited William of Orange - James' son-in-law - to come and take over. *(Well, if you lived in Holland and were offered England, what would <u>you</u> do? No contest, my dear! Ethel.)* James took the hint and hot-foot it into exile to France *(best place for him. Ethel.)* where he died in 1701.

WILLIAM III
1688-1702
(With MARY, died 1694)

William III - or rather William of Orange as he was known after the Dutch royal house *(or because he rather fancied Nell Gwynne. Ethel.)* - agreed to the English throne simply because he thought it would help him contain French expansion. He was not a well-loved King, but Mary was. Apart from the Massacre of Glencoe in 1692 *(in which 38 Macdonalds were consumed in record time by the Cambells, hence the reason for wearing kilts to more quickly dissipate the gaseous results of such greed and gluttony. Ethel.)* and the odd scrap with the French, William's reign is best known for the Battle of the Boyne, which set the scene of Irish politics and government for centuries. William was succeeded by his sister-in-law, Anne, the last of the Stuarts.

THE BATTLE OF THE BOYNE 1690

Before Henry VIII declared himself King of Ireland in 1541, English rule had been restricted to the area around Dublin called The Pale. Elizabeth I and James I extended this by sending over Protestant settlers who quickly gained a numerical ascendancy over the native Catholic population. When James II was deposed by William III, the Irish Catholics sided with James *(natch, as he was a Catholic. Clear so far? Ethel.)* and the Ulster Protestants sided with William *(ditto Protestant. Ethel.)*. William actually tried to grant better terms to Irish Catholics, but the Protestant-dominated Irish Parliament ignored them and issued its own Penal Laws that effectively turned the Catholic population into second-class citizens.

William had had enough! After the siege of Londonderry (when 30,000 Protestants took refuge from Irish Catholics behind the city walls before being relieved by the English navy) William fielded an army which met with James' forces at the River Boyne and thrashed him. The slightly confusing fact is that William was, of course, James' son-in-law, so rather stupidly turned a blind eye and let him slip away back into exile *(however, the alternative would have been to top his own father-in-law, which may not have been terribly clever in terms of enjoying what was left of his married life. Ethel.)*

ANNE
1702-1714

The key event of Anne's reign was the War of the Spanish Succession, started by the French *(as ever! Ethel.)* claiming the empty Spanish throne for themselves. England declared war on France in 1702, and through the efforts of the Duke of Marlborough, won stunning victories against the French at Blenheim *(1-0! Ethel.)*, Ramillies *(2-0! Ethel)*, Oudenarde *(3-0! Ethel.)* and Malplaquet *(4-0! Ethel.)*. In addition, England captured Gibralter, expelled the French from the Netherlands and captured Minorca. Peace was declared at the Treaty of Utrecht in 1713.

Anne also presided over the Act of Union in 1707, which ended Scottish independence and abolished the Scottish Parliament. *(And talking about Acts of Union, Anne had no less than eighteen children and died exhausted at the age of 49. She died, however, without an heir, which is unusual, as most paintings of that time show her with a full head of it. Ethel.)*

Anne will chiefly be remembered for Queen Anne furniture, so called because it has, like her, spindly but well-turned legs.

THE HANOVERIANS
1714-1910

GEORGE I	1714-1727
GEORGE II	1727-1760
GEORGE III	1760-1820
GEORGE IV	1820-1830
WILLIAM IV	1830-1837
VICTORIA	1837-1901
EDWARD VII	1901-1910

The Stuart line died out because the Act of Succession *(remember children? Ethel.)* specifically denied the throne to Catholics. A hasty trawl through the family tree dug up an old biddy called Sophie, the Protestant Electress of Hanover, a grand daughter of James I. But damn it all if she didn't go and pop her clogs that very same year, leaving the throne to her son, George I, the first of the Hanoverians.

THE PROTESTING
ELECTRESS

GEORGE I
1714-1727

George I had everything required to become King of England. He was dull and dim-witted, he spoke no English (and his new subjects spoke no German), he came from a landlocked country so understood nothing about maritime matters on which much of England's wealth was built - and last but not least, he was German!

Within a year there was a Jacobite rising in Scotland when the 'Old Pretender' James Edward Stuart, the son of the late James II, attempted the English throne. This was easily put down, and after that things just seemed to drift along at a pretty pace. Daniel Defoe published Robinson Crusoe *(it came out on a Friday, as I recall. Ethel.)* and Jonathan Swift published Gulliver's Travels. George I didn't even have the decency to *die* in this country, expiring instead in Hanover at the age of 67. George I was a *good* German.

GEORGE II
1727-1760

Was George II any better than the prototype? Certainly a lot more happened in his reign, and he *did* speak English. The first Jacobite rising of 1715 was followed in 1745 by the son of the Old Pretender, the

---

BONNY PRINCE CHARLIE

The revolt by the Old Pretender having failed so miserably in 1715, it fell to the Old Pretender's son, the Young Pretender Charles Edward Stuart, the grandson of James II, to try again in 1745. He had slightly more success at first, capturing Edinburgh and beating an English army at Prestonpans. But that was about as good as it got. For some strange reason *(precisely. What on earth is there to do in Edinburgh? Ethel.)* Charles dallied too long in Edinburgh, and when he at last sallied out he was well and truly thrashed at the Battle of Culloden in 1746. Charles fled the field and was hidden on the Scottish islands before taking ship to France. *(He died a sad and drunk old man in Rome in 1788 in a windowless room, humming his favourite ditty: 'Oh to see the sky.' Ethel.)*

Young Pretender *(remember you have to keep it simple for the Scots. Ethel.)*. This, too, led to failure and the rise of the myth of Bonny Prince Charlie.

Overseas, George's position as Elector of Hanover got England involved in the War of Austrian Succession, 1740-1748, *(War of Spanish Succession, War of Austrian Succession. Why can't these Johnny Foreigners sort out their own successors? Ethel.)* and the Seven Years' War of 1756-1763, both giving us yet another chance to wup the French *(ah, so some good did come from it, then. Ethel.)*.

George II himself led his troops at the Battle of Dettingen in 1743, which threw the French out of Germany, the last time a British King led an army into battle.

GEORGE III
1760-1820

George III, of course, was by far the best of the Hanoverians *(on the male side, anyway. Ethel.)* and had a jolly good reign, helped along as he was by the Duke of Wellington and Lord Nelson.

THE BUILDING OF AN EMPIRE

England already had colonies in America, Canada, India and the West Indies by this time, but now was a time of enormous growth. The French were thrown out of Canada by General James Woolfe's victory at Quebec in 1759, while Clive had secured Bengal at the Battle of Plassey in 1757. The Treaty of Paris in 1763 then gave England more West Indian islands, and all in all, everything in the kitchen was looking rather tidy *(or is that everything in the garden was looking rather rosy? I can never remember. Ethel.)*.

The British Empire reached its most powerful during the reign of Victoria, taking in India, Africa, Australia and New Zealand, the West Indies and Canada. *(And of course now we've got nothing: not even Calais! Ethel.)*

He also went mad from time to time, and he also lost us our American colonies, but that's another story.

The Napoleonic Wars played the major role in his time, when a Corsican, Napoleon Bonaparte, thought he could take over the world. In the end, however, all he took over was the Island of St. Helena, where he famously died in 1821.

THE BATTLE OF TRAFALGAR 1805

This of course is where Lord Nelson met his death after having asked Hardy for one final snog. At Trafalgar, the combined French and Spanish fleets of 33 ships of the line were met and defeated by 27 British ships. The normal battle format in those days was for two fleets to sail parallel and beat crap out of each other until something *(a mast, a sail, the captain, whatever. Ethel.)* fell off or sank or indeed surrendered or went home for tea. Nelson, however, had other plans, and famously drove straight at the enemy ships in two columns, 'breaking the line' as they say and winning his famous victory. Nelson's body was immersed in a cask of brandy for the journey home. *(Not <u>Napoleon</u> brandy, I trust? Ethel.)*

In between times, ie. from 1793 to 1815 with a little break between 1802 and 1803 for tea and sandwiches, the French tricolour flew from as many flagpoles around the world as there are runs in a tart's stockings.

But as with all wars, initial successes soon become stalemates, which soon become retreats and final defeat. In Napoleon's case, and with the help of allies, it was Wellington's land victories that started

AMERICAN WAR OF
INDEPENDENCE 1775-1783

It was all Woolfe's fault, of course, for throwing the French out of Canada. While they were there, the 13 American colonies needed England's protection against the French, and when they'd gone, they didn't. *(England was also taxing the bottom out of the colonists, but that is of minor importance, naturally. Ethel.)*

The Colonists argued 'No taxation without representation', and when that was ignored the fisticuffs started in earnest *(well, actually in Lexington and Concord. Ethel.)* It was French intervention on the American side, with army and fleet, that finally led to English surrender at Yorktown in 1781 and a realisation that the war could not be won. *(Those bloody French again! Just like French knickers - one Yank and they're off! Ethel.)*

in Portugal and drove the French armies back through Spain and into France, and Nelson's stunning sea victories at the Nile, Copenhagen and Trafalgar that gave England control of the seas.

The final battle at Waterloo crushed French power and restored peace in Europe *(for at least a week or two, anyway. Ethel.)*.

THE BATTLE OF WATERLOO 1815

Ten years after Trafalgar gave England total command of the seas, Napoleon met his match on the battlefield of Waterloo, where he was roundly beaten by a combined force of English, Belgium and Hanoverian troops led by Wellington, and a Prussian army led by Blucher. When the French contingent pulled into the Eurostar terminal at Waterloo, the combined forces of Wellington and Blucher refused to let them leave the train and sent them packing without so much as a 'by your leave' or a cup of British Rail tea. Three carriage loads of French soldiers were also found not to have proper tickets and had to pay a penalty fare. *(I think that's fare enough, don't you? Ethel.)*

The French have never forgiven us for this, and even to this day refuse to answer you in English, even when you shout really really loudly at them.

GEORGE IV
1820-1830

George III spent the last nine years of his life blind
and a total loony, with the Price of Wales as Regent.
On George's death he became George IV. For a
reign lasting ten years, he achieved very little except
a procession of mistresses. He also famously agreed
to marry Caroline of Brunswick so that Parliament
would pay off his huge debts, only to accuse her of
adultery and exclude her from his Coronation. In
the last year of his reign he granted political rights of
Catholics, and died a very fat man at Windsor. *(A
decade of decadence, then! Ethel.)*

WILLIAM IV
1830-1837

William was George III's third son, so didn't expect
to become King, which he did at the age of 64, his
middle brother having rather selfishly turned his
toes in 1827. During a period of intense change and
reform and new legislation *(indeed one wonders whether
they were called William simply because they seem to preside
over a lot of Bills. Ethel.)*,

William is generally thought to have acquitted himself rather well, if not a little dully. Like his brother he also had money problems, and he also dumped his mistress of 22 years (and the mother of his 10 illegitimate children) to marry Princess Adelaide of Saxe-Meiningen in 1818 to boost his coffers. *(So, from Sex-my darling to Saxe-Meiningen to Save-my money, eh? Ethel.)*

VICTORIA
1837-1901

She ruled for 63 years over the world's greatest Empire and oversaw a social and economic revolution in England that made it one of the world's richest countries *(apart from all the poor people in it, of course. Ethel.)*. She married Prince Albert of Saxe-Coburg and went into lifelong mourning when he died early of typhoid. *(It was his own fault. He was told to aphoid wearing ties. Ethel.)* Paintings of her as a young women show her as slim and attractive, while photographs, which only came in later on in her life, show her as a bit of a fat old frump. *(But then cameras these days can lie as well as the rest of us, can they not? Ethel.)*

During her reign the Penny Post was introduced, smallpox vaccination and primary education both became compulsory and the Salvation Army was born *(so she was responsible for those blasted bands! Ethel.)*. Voting rights became more widespread, trade unions were legalised and Alfred organised the Great Exhibition of 1851 that gave England a worldwide showcase.

On the Empire front, Canada became the first independent dominion in the Empire, and the Boer War *(you can guess why that was so-called, yawn. Ethel.)* came and went, as did the Crimean War, which famously gave us the Balaclava Helmet, the Cardigan, the Charge of the Light Brigade and Florence Nightingale *(so called after the time of day, the length of time taken and the weather conditions prevailing at her conception. Ethel.)* Gordon of Khartoum also died rather famously at the hands of a Dervish horde, and the place was later renamed Gordontomb.

There was also a bit of trouble in India, where a Mutiny broke out in 1857 after native soldiers (sepoys) spread the word by passing chapattis (small and flat unleavened bread) all over the country as a signal. At one point the sepoys thought they could win *(ie they were obviously on a roll. Ethel.)*, but the Mutiny was quelled and India passed out of the control of the East India

Company and became part of the Empire proper.

(It is interesting to note that, after independence, Indians got their own back for the nationwide network of Eel, Pie and Mash shops set up by English restaurateurs by setting up a similar network of curry houses across the British Isles. On a grammatical note, and for those who peruse Indian menus, 'Vinda' is the Hindi word for the phrase 'There will definitely be the sound of an angry flock of seagulls in the ...' Ethel.)

Victoria died in 1901 at the ripe old age of 81, and with her passed the golden Victorian age. After that could only come mediocrity.

EDWARD VII
1901-1910

He didn't come to the throne until he was 59, and he was never trusted all that much by his mother. *(I have always maintained that men should <u>never</u> be fully trusted! Ethel.)* He was thought a good King, however, and presided over the granting of dominion status to both Australia and New Zealand and the signing of the Entente Cordiale between Britain and France and the Triple Entente between Britain, France and Russia *(so who the hell signed the Double Entendre? Or did it have no meaning? Ethel.)*

The Wright Brothers made the first manned flight *(which turned out to be plain sailing after all that fuss. Ethel.)* and Mrs Pankhurst formed the Suffragette Movement *(and whose antics gave us the phrase 'Hanky Panky'. Ethel.)*

Edward died after a lifetime of slim mistresses and fat cigars *(or vice versa, with the emphasis very much on the vice! Ethel.)*, the last Hanoverian.

THE HOUSE OF WINDSOR 1910-

GEORGE V	1910-1936
EDWARD VIII	1936-
ABDICATED	
GEORGE VI	1936-1952
ELIZABETH II	1952-

George's family name was Saxe-Coburg-Gotha, a very German-sounding name, and one he swiftly changed halfway through England's war with Germany in 1914-1918. Because he lived at Windsor, he chose that name *(thank God he didn't live in Chipping Sodbury! Ethel.)*.

GEORGE V
1910-1936

Happily married to May of Tek *(if she'd been any taller she'd have been known as High Tech. Ethel)*, who ruled with him as Queen Mary, George V was a very popular King indeed, and helped maintain the dignity of the Crown through World War I, the Partition of Ireland and numerous other Government and constitutional crises.

A famous phrase of George V, when he refused to convalesce any longer at Bognor Regis after a long illness, preferring Windsor Castle instead, was 'Bugger Bognor' *(but despite an extensive search, they were never able to find the chap. Ethel.)*. George V was also an avid stamp collector *(presumably on the premise that 'philately will get you everywhere'. Ethel.)*.

The First World War lasted from 1914 to 1918, and kicked off with the assassination of Arch Duke Ferdinand, the Austrian heir to the throne, in Serbia by one Gavrilo Princips *(not English, then, even though his name is an anagram of 'Spoil virgin crap'! Ethel.)*. Germany invaded France through Belgium, England and the Empire went to help Belgium, Russia got involved, then the Americans.

In three and a half years of trench warfare, the line called the Western Front advanced no more than 15 kilometres in either direction *(an early version of the M25, then. Ethel.)*. In 1918, they all met in a railway carriage, shook hands and went home.

In Ireland, there was the Easter Egg Rising of 1918 *(caused by a shortage of Belgian chocolate because the Germans had eaten it all. Ethel.)* which led in 1920-21 to the partition of the country into The Irish Free State in the South and the Irish Slightly More Expensive State in the North.

In Government, the 1918 Reform Act gave the vote to women over 30 but as no woman will ever admit to being over 30, they had to lower the age to 21 in 1928. The first Labour Government was formed in 1924, but disbanded nine months later when the Labour was over. A Great Depression also spread across the country in 1931, but free counselling on a massive scale and a lot of post-traumatic stress therapy eventually cured the problem and put a smile back on people's faces.

George V celebrated his Silver Jubilee on the throne *(something he ate, apparently. Ethel.)* and died a year later in 1936.

EDWARD VIII
1936-ABDICATION

George V knew his own son so well that he prophesied "That boy will ruin himself in 12 months after I'm dead." In fact it took him exactly that amount of time, from coming to the throne in January to abdicating the following December to marry the twice-divorced Mrs Wallace Simpson. *(What on earth could she offer Edward that England couldn't? Perhaps you'd better not tell me! Ethel.)*

A key event of his reign was the maiden voyage of the Queen Mary *(presumably because she wasn't allowed to do it while her husband George V was still alive. Ethel.)*

GEORGE VI
1936-1952

The second son of George V was a much better proposition for King of England, and with Queen Elizabeth *(now the Queen Mother, because she's the Mother of our current Queen, stupid. Ethel.)* helped lead his people through the ravages of World War II and the damage caused by his brother's abdication.

Edward VIII's Titanic abdication.

"The figurehead was Simpson instead,
Sucking up to the rich and famous."

In 1938 Prime Minister Neville Chamberlain brought back a piece of paper from his meeting with Hitler in Germany *(it's all they had in duty-free. Ethel)* where he agreed that Hitler could take over a piece of Czechoslovakia if that was all he'd take. *(It was widely applauded on his return as 'A Piece in Our Time'. Ethel.)*

Hitler obviously wasn't concentrating, because in 1938 he took over the *whole* of Czechoslovakia, and when he stormed into Poland a year later war broke out. Winston Churchill became Prime Minister in 1940 and his famous 'fight them on the beaches' speech worried the Germans so much that they decided to fight the Battle of Britain in the air instead, but even that didn't work. Of course, if Hitler had had the right connections, as did George I, he could have just come in and been King no problem. *(Perhaps that's what made him so much of a sour Kraut. Ethel.)*

As with World War I, Son of World War I raged on and on, all over the world, with Germany taking on everybody and eventually getting well and truly thrashed when everyone turned on them.

In the East, the Japanese, after early successes, finally bombed out in 1945 and peace returned to these islands once again.

ELIZABETH II
1952-

One of the longest-reigning monarchs, Queen Elizabeth II is named after a famous cruise liner. She has seen Britain withdraw from a quarter of the world as she has granted independence to her former colonies, keeping only Gibralter *(probably because it pisses the Spanish off. Ethel.)* and the Falklands *(ditto Argentina. Ethel.)*.

The Cold War occupied most of England's military energies until the fall of Communism in the early 1990s, since when the thrust has changed to the growth of Muslim Fundamentalism across Asia and the near East. *(Where does Saddam Hussein keep his CDs? In a rack! Ethel.)*

"Once more into their breeches, dear friends, once more."

The Queen has four children, and it is estimated at the time of writing that the Crown of England will pass to her eldest son, Prince Charles. This will be a good thing because he talks to plants and vegetables, and the majority of England's population is now made up of couch potatoes.

It will be a *good match*.

THE END
(so far! Ethel.)

Are you still Barking Mad?

Yes? Then if you have enjoyed this irreverent look at the History of England, please find out about other titles in the Dog's range, specifically the eight volumes of the Freddie Farquar 'Naughty but Nice!' series. These are all A6 hardbacks, 64 pages in length and illustrated in full-colour throughout. Titles are:

Bawdy & Risqué Stories (Available now)
A 'recently discovered' cornucopia of 50-plus fine Edwardian bawdy humorous stories. A rich seam for those who like to read and tell a good rude story.
ISBN 0 9533582 3 2

The Ballad of Eskimo Nell (Available now)
The adventures of Eskimo Nell. One of the greatest naughty rhymes of all time, this new and richly illustrated edition does this old masterpiece full justice.
ISBN 0 9533582 0 8

How To Tell She's Blonde, (even in the dark) (Available now)
It's not that hard! The most superbly distilled and illustrated collection of Blondie girlie jokes ever, this special edition swings all ways.
ISBN 0 9533582 2 4

'Ladies of the Night' Calling Cards (Available now)
A remarkable collection of genuine 'working girl' call-box cards. Pithy and funny comments abound in this rollicking tour of 'alternative' advertising.
ISBN 0 9533582 1 6

Why Chocolate is Better Than Sex (Publishing 2000)
A must for those who'd rather get messy in bed with a good old
box of rich Belgian choccies than a good old rich Belgian! Made
for choccy luvvies everywhere!
ISBN 0 9533582 6 7

Why Women are Superior to Men (Publishing 2000)
The book half the population's been waiting for! Compiled by
women who simply cannot understand why there was ever an
element of doubt!
ISBN 0 9533582 7 5

Why We Love (to throttle) Lawyers   (Publishing 2000)
A closer-than-close look at the oldest profession. This book
reinforces our natural prejudices yet still remains the best ever
present for any you know!
ISBN 0 9533582 4 0

Essential Golfing Stories   (Publishing 2000)
The last male bastion revealed! The only place you can spend
time with swingers without the wife getting mad. Full of
fabulous golfing stories.
ISBN 0 9533582 5 9

You can purchase by credit card direct from our website:

www.dogs-rollocks.com

or send or fax your order to

The Dog's Rollocks Ideas Co Ltd.,
Timbers, Milford Road, Elstead, Godalming, Surrey GU8 6HZ.
Tel/Fax: +44 (0) 1252 702754

ORIGINAL PETER SEARLE CARTOON ILLUSTRATIONS

If you would like signed prints of any of the illustrations in this book, they are available printed full-size on A4 (they are reproduced in this book at under half size) in sets of four.

A set of four is available at just £17.50 the set, printed on top-quality 300gsm art paper and individually signed by the artist.

HOW TO ORDER

To order, simply write the relevant page numbers on a sheet of paper and post to The Dog's Rollocks Ideas Co Ltd. at the address shown on the back cover, complete with cheque/PO payment made payable to The Dog's Rollocks Ideas Co Ltd.

Postage and packing to all UK addresses is free of charge. Please add £2.50 to all orders for delivery outside the UK.